EARTH'S
HISTORY
THROUGH
ROCKS

REEFS AND VOLCANOES

HOW EARTH'S ATOLLS FORMED

KATHLEEN A. KLATTE

PowerKiDS
press
New York

Published in 2020 by The Rosen Publishing Group, Inc.
29 East 21st Street, New York, NY 10010

First Edition

Editor: Sarah Machajewski
Book Design: Tanya Dellaccio

Photo Credits: Cover Neal Wilson/Moment/Getty Images; p. 5 Dani Vincek/Shutterstock.com; p. 7 (Cape Verde) Susana_Martins/Shutterstock.com; p. 7 (Charles Darwin) https://upload.wikimedia. org/wikipedia/commons/1/18/Charles_Darwin_by_G._Richmond.png; p. 9 (Vila Franca do Campo) De Visu/Shutterstock.com; p. 9 (basalt rock) arka38/Shutterstock.com; p. 9 (obsidian rock) Bjoern Wylezich/Shutterstock.com; p. 11 (Mauna Kea) Galyna Andrushko/Shutterstock.com; p. 11 (Samoa Islands) Martin Valigursky/Shutterstock.com; p. . 13 (top) Cingular/Shutterstock.com; p. 13 (bottom) Hamizan Yusof/Shutterstock.com; p. 14 Edward Haylan/Shutterstock.com; p. 15 lavizzara/Shutterstock. com; p. 17 Kevin J. Frost/Shutterstock.com; p. 19 Siraphob Werakijpanich/Shutterstock.com; p. 21 (HMS *Beagle*) Bettmann/Getty Images; pp. 21 (coral reef), Photo 12/Universal Images Group/Getty Images; p. 22 https://upload.wikimedia.org/wikipedia/commons/c/ce/Alexandre_Agassiz._Portrait_Wellcome_ M0016605_%28cropped%29.jpg; p. 23 The Asahi Shimbun Premium/The Asahi Shimbun/Getty Images; p. 25 Sylvain CORDIER/Gamma-Rapho/Getty Images; p. 27 (top) Universal Images Group/Universal Images Group Editorial/Getty Images; p. 27 (bottom) Pascale Gueret/Shutterstock.com; p. 29 Stocktrek Images/Getty Images; p. 30 RWBrooks/Shutterstock.com.

Library of Congress Cataloging-in-Publication Data

Names: Klatte, Kathleen A., author.
Title: Reefs and volcanoes : how Earth's atolls formed / Kathleen A. Klatte.
Description: New York : PowerKids Press, [2020] | Series: Earth's history through rocks | Includes index.
Identifiers: LCCN 2018050271| ISBN 9781725301603 (pbk.) | ISBN 9781725301627 (library bound) | ISBN 9781725301610 (6 pack)
Subjects: LCSH: Coral reefs and islands–Juvenile literature. | Islands–Juvenile literature. | Volcanoes–Juvenile literature.
Classification: LCC GB461 .K53 2020 | DDC 551.42/4–dc23
LC record available at https://lccn.loc.gov/2018050271

Manufactured in the United States of America

CPSIA Compliance Information: Batch #CSPK19. For Further Information contact Rosen Publishing, New York, New York at 1-800-237-9932.

CONTENTS

WHAT IS AN ATOLL?

What is a reef? A volcano? An island? And how do they come together to form an atoll? An atoll is a ring of coral surrounding a lagoon. Atolls are the result of geological and biological processes and take millions of years to form. Atolls are always changing.

Some atolls are barely visible above the sea. Before the invention of tools such as **sonar**, this caused many shipwrecks. Other atolls—such as those that make up the Maldives—are large enough for people to live on them. Atolls have fascinated sailors, **naturalists**, and scientists for centuries. Although geologists and other scientists had theories about how atolls formed, the **technology** to really understand the process didn't exist until the 20th century.

GEOLOGISTS

Scientists who study rocks to learn about Earth are called geologists. They can learn about things that happened long ago by studying the minerals and the fossilized plants and animals found in different types of rock. Geologists often study events that happened thousands or even millions of years ago.

The Maldives, shown here, is a country in the Indian Ocean made up of 26 atolls!

EVER-CHANGING EARTH

Earth is always changing. It renews and rebuilds itself. Have you ever built something out of blocks and then taken it apart and built something new from the pieces? Earth does that, too.

Atolls form following several kinds of changes that happen together—some building up, some breaking down. Volcanoes create new layers of rock. Wind, water, and wildlife deposit material, or matter, on top of the volcanic rock. Living things settle onto that land. Over time, wind, weather, and waves break the rock down into sand through a process called erosion.

Sometimes, land sinks into the sea. Reefs surrounding the land continue to grow around it. As the reefs grow larger and form a circle around the sunken land, an atoll takes shape.

In the Cape Verde Islands, Darwin observed seashells fossilized in rock high in the mountains. This suggests that the mountainside was once the bottom of the sea. ▶

CHARLES DARWIN

In the 1830s, an English naturalist named Charles Darwin set out on an **expedition** on a ship called the HMS *Beagle*. Darwin, who was born in 1809, visited many different places during the *Beagle's* voyage. He studied many plants, animals, and rocks. In his travels, Darwin observed how an earthquake could raise up parts of the land and bury others. Darwin had many ideas about how Earth changes, including thoughts on how atolls form.

UNDERWATER VOLCANOES

A volcano begins with a hot spot in Earth's crust. Molten rock, called lava, erupts through cracks in the ocean floor. When the lava comes into contact with seawater, it cools and forms solid rock. One of the most common types of underwater lava is called pillow lava.

After thousands of years and thousands of eruptions, enough layers of rock collect to form a seamount, or underwater mountain. Underwater volcanoes form new landmasses at a rate of about an inch (2.5 cm) a year.

Did you know that most of the deep ocean floor is made of lava flows? That's because there are more active volcanoes on the ocean floor than on land. Many are located along mid-ocean ridges—places where the edges of the plates that form Earth's crust come together.

READING THE ROCKS

ROCK FORMED FROM COOLED LAVA IS CALLED IGNEOUS ROCK. TWO OF THE MOST COMMON TYPES ARE BASALT AND OBSIDIAN.

ISLAND FORMED FROM UNDERWATER VOLCANO, PORTUGAL

BASALT

OBSIDIAN

Basalt is a common type of igneous rock with a very rough appearance. Obsidian is smooth and glassy.

VOLCANIC ISLANDS

When a volcano becomes tall enough to rise above the ocean's surface, it forms a volcanic island. Some of the tallest mountains in the world are actually volcanic islands. When measured from base to **summit**, these islands often are taller than mountains found on land, even Mount Everest.

Mauna Kea, a volcano in Hawaii, is the tallest sea mountain in the world and one of the tallest mountains of any kind on Earth. It last erupted thousands of years ago.

Sometimes, volcanic islands grow large enough for people to live on them. Despite the dangers of living near a volcano that might erupt, many volcanic islands are inhabited. Some examples are Hawaii, the Philippine Islands, the islands of Indonesia, the Galápagos Islands, the Samoan Islands, and New Zealand.

This photo shows a volcanic beach on one of the Samoan Islands in the South Pacific.

ROCK OR PLANT?

What we call coral isn't actually a rock or a plant, even though it can look like both. It's the hardened shells or skeletons left behind by tiny creatures called coral polyps, which can resemble underwater flowers. Over time, their skeletons bond together to form reefs, which have stonelike qualities.

Most coral polyps require sunlight and warm, shallow water to survive. A reef begins to form when coral polyps settle onto the underwater rock surrounding an island. Each polyp is tiny by itself, but they live in colonies, which allows them to create large coral reefs.

Most coral grows about an inch (2.5 cm) a year. Coral has growth rings, just like trees. Geologists can study these growth rings to learn what Earth was like hundreds of years ago.

IMPORTANT ECOSYSTEMS

Coral reefs are home to some of the most diverse ecosystems in the world. Plants anchor to the surfaces of reefs formed by coral exoskeletons. The coral structure helps form calm places in the sea for young fish and plants to grow, as well as places to hide from predators.

These tiny star-shaped structures aren't plants. They're a colony of tiny animals!

READING THE ROCKS

MANY CORAL EXOSKELETONS CONTAIN CALCIUM CARBONATE, A MINERAL THAT'S ALSO FOUND IN PEARLS AND THE SHELLS OF OTHER MARINE ANIMALS.

CORAL REEFS

The most common types of coral reefs are fringing reefs and barrier reefs. A fringing reef is one that grows off the coast of a landmass, forming a small lagoon between the shoreline and the open sea. The reef shelters the lagoon, making a good home for plants and young animals.

A barrier reef is larger, forming a much wider and deeper lagoon between the coast and the reef. Some barrier reefs are visible above water, but others aren't. This used to be very dangerous for sailing ships. It's very common for reefs to be surrounded by shipwrecks, some of them centuries old.

Sometimes, when a reef breaks the surface of the ocean, enough dirt and other matter collect on top of the coral to form an island. Over time, enough soil may build up to support plant life.

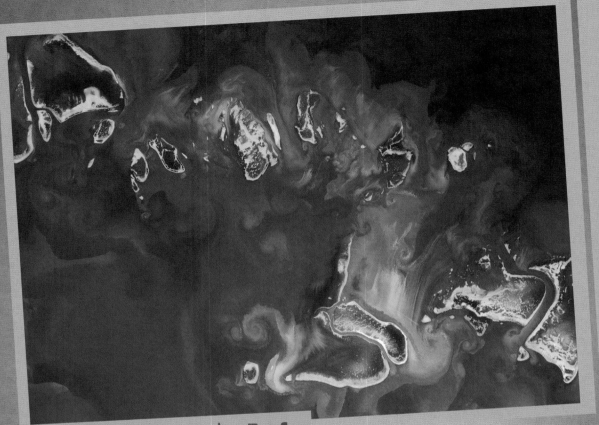

The Great Barrier Reef
can be seen from space!

THE GREAT BARRIER REEF

The Great Barrier Reef, located off Queensland, Australia, is the largest coral reef on Earth. The reef is about 500,000 years old, but its size and shape have changed over time. It's home to an amazing variety of fish, reptiles, marine mammals, and birds.

AN ATOLL AT LAST

How do all these geological elements come together to form an atoll? It takes many years for an atoll to grow. The process begins when a barrier reef forms around a volcanic island, surrounding it completely.

Volcanoes (and volcanic islands) don't last forever. An underwater volcano can move off a hot spot due to shifts in the plates that make up Earth's crust. A volcano that hasn't erupted in the last 10,000 years but could erupt again is called a dormant volcano. A volcano that hasn't erupted in 10,000 years and shows no signs of erupting again is considered extinct.

When a volcano stops erupting and building up new layers of rock, natural forces such as wind, rain, and ocean waves begin the process of erosion. A volcano can also collapse and sink into the sea.

READING THE ROCKS

EARTH IS ALWAYS CHANGING, AND SOMETIMES A VOLCANO THAT HAS BEEN CLASSIFIED AS EXTINCT CAN STILL ERUPT.

This is an extinct volcano on the island of Rarotonga, the largest of the Cook Islands in the South Pacific Ocean.

When the volcanic rock has sunk completely beneath the water, leaving the ring of coral in place, an atoll forms. The space in the center of the coral, where the island used to be, becomes a lagoon. Some lagoons have an outlet to the sea, while others are completely enclosed. The reef protects the waters of the lagoon, providing a safe place for an amazing variety of marine plants and animals.

Atolls can form islands large enough to support human life. **Tourism** is often the main type of business on these islands. People travel from all over the world to photograph the wonderful scenery and wildlife. Diving among the shipwrecks that often surround atolls is also a popular activity.

People travel from all over the world to visit the Maldives. ▶

THE MALDIVES

The Maldives is a country located entirely on a chain of atolls. It's made up of about 1,200 coral islands. Tourism is one of its major industries, along with fishing.

DARWIN'S THEORY

Atolls have fascinated people for centuries. As scientists began to learn more about Earth and how different living things survive, atolls puzzled them. They wondered how there could be rings of coral far out in the open ocean, since coral requires warm, shallow water and sunlight to grow.

In 1837, during his trip around the world on the HMS *Beagle*, Charles Darwin visited many different island chains. He theorized that atolls formed when coral grew up around a volcanic island that was sinking back into the sea. Since there was no way at the time to prove or disprove Darwin's theory, it was accepted until a different idea could be suggested. It would be a century before scientists could confirm that Darwin's theory of atoll formation is correct.

Darwin traveled around the world and made many discoveries about life on Earth. The knowledge he uncovered helped advance science in a big way.

AGASSIZ'S THEORY

In the 1870s, a geologist named Alexander Agassiz suggested a different theory. He thought that atolls formed from large coral islands. He theorized that over time, the reefs grew so large and heavy that the coral in the center died off, leaving the distinctive ring that forms an atoll.

In 1881, Darwin suggested drilling through an atoll to see whose theory was correct. If the atoll was rooted in volcanic rock, Darwin was right. If scientists found sand, Agassiz was right. In the 1890s, the Royal Society of London made three attempts to drill through Funafuti Atoll in Tuvalu, in the South Pacific. However, Darwin had underestimated the size of the reefs that form an atoll. The machinery of the time wasn't able to drill through the coral to see what was beneath it.

ALEXANDER AGASSIZ

SCIENTIFIC THEORY

A theory is an idea to explain how something works. If there is enough evidence to support the theory, it's accepted until it can be proven or disproven.

This is Funafuti Atoll, where scientists first attempted to prove Darwin's theory

A DANGEROUS PLACE TO LIVE?

The surfaces of many atolls aren't far above sea level. This means they're affected by many changes in climate and water level.

Global warming is an increase in the temperature of the atmosphere and oceans. It's thought to be the result of air pollution caused by humans. Global warming affects everyone, but people living along the coasts and on islands suffer the most. As the polar ice caps continue to melt and sea levels continue to rise, the coasts of low-lying islands flood.

Natural disasters can also negatively affect island communities. Tsunamis, which are enormous waves caused by underwater earthquakes, flood coastline communities and are powerful enough to destroy buildings. Seawater from flooding **contaminates** the freshwater that people, plants, and animals need to live.

Tsunamis that hit atolls can cause a lot of destruction. For example, a tsunami that hit the Midway Atoll in 2011 flooded bird nests and burrows across the island. The birds took years to recover from the impact.

READING THE ROCKS

CORAL BLEACHING IS A THREAT CAUSED BY WARMING OCEAN TEMPERATURES. WHEN WATER WARMS, CORAL GETS RID OF THE ALGAE LIVING IN ITS TISSUES AND TURNS WHITE. WHILE THE CORAL ISN'T DEAD, IT BECOMES STRESSED AND IS AT GREATER RISK OF DYING.

TESTS AND TECHNOLOGY

In the 1940s and 1950s, the U.S. Atomic Energy Commission **detonated** bombs in the Marshall Islands to study the effects on land, air, and water. One test proved Darwin's theory correct when the Enewetak Atoll was found to be resting on volcanic rock. Other outcomes weren't so great. Bombs destroyed entire islands, and water and plants on others are still **radioactive**. However, the coral has made a remarkable recovery.

WHO LIVES ON ATOLLS?

Migratory birds use atolls to rest during long flights. They also build nests and lay eggs on the islands. Their droppings carry seeds and organic matter that help build up the soil. Coconut crabs, which begin their lives in the sea, come ashore on atolls to live and eat the coconuts that grow there—along with whatever else comes their way! The waters surrounding atolls are also home to many varieties of fish, sea mammals, sea turtles, and much more.

People have lived on atolls for centuries. Since the soil of many of these islands doesn't contain enough **nutrients** to grow common food crops, fishing has been the main source of food, work, and trade on many atolls. Tuna fish and coconut trees are the most common food sources. They feature in the ancient stories of the Maldives.

A bridled tern, a migratory bird, relaxes on a beach in French Polynesia. Birds such as the bridled tern use atolls as resting points during their long migrations.

ATOLLS TODAY

Today, some people who live on small atolls catch and raise just enough to feed themselves. Larger atolls, such as those found in the nations of Kiribati and the Maldives, have resorts, or large hotel properties. Tourism is one of their main trades. Other atolls are protected places where no one can fish, hunt, or live. Scientists go there to study the geology and wildlife.

Scientists today don't even have to set foot on an atoll to study some of its geological features. Tools such as sonar and radar can measure the depth and **density** of islands and reefs. Images taken from space show how landmasses change in shape and size over time. NASA's Goddard Space Flight Center is a place where research about Earth is conducted via satellites.

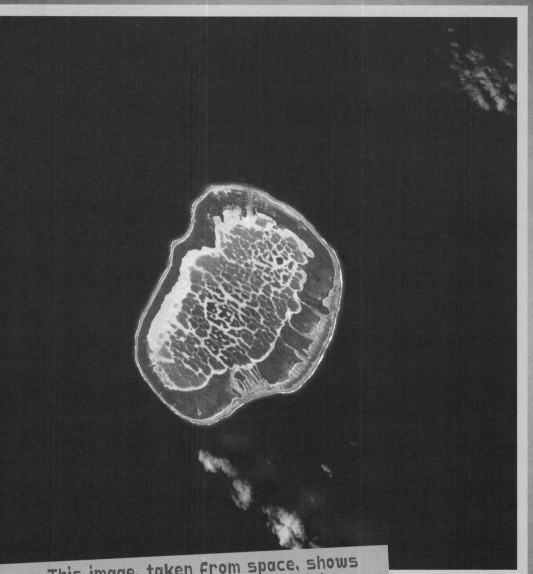

This image, taken from space, shows Mataiva Atoll in the South Pacific.

A DYNAMIC SYSTEM

The systems that form atolls are always changing, but they work in balance. The actions of people can change this balance. Global warming has caused sea levels to rise. As the coasts become flooded, landmass decreases. Rising water temperatures can kill coral. Chemicals that people dump into the water can also kill coral.

To protect the natural wonders of Earth's atolls, many countries have laws to keep them safe. In Micronesia, where tourism is a main industry, people practice ecotourism. This is a system in which the places people visit are designed to recycle resources and have as little impact on the planet as possible. With greater care for how people treat our planet, Earth will continue to create beautiful atolls for centuries to come.

GLOSSARY

contaminate: To pollute something, such as drinking water, so it's unusable to people or animals.

density: The amount of matter or things in a given area.

detonate: To explode or cause to explode.

diverse: Different or varied.

exoskeleton: The hard outer covering of an animal's body.

expedition: A journey undertaken by a group of people for a particular purpose.

migratory: Taking part in migration, or the movement of animals from one place to another as the seasons change.

naturalist: A person who studies plants and animals as they live in nature.

nutrient: Something taken in by a plant or animal that helps it grow and stay healthy.

radioactive: Putting out harmful energy in the form of tiny particles.

sonar: A machine that uses sound waves to find things in a body of water.

summit: The highest point of a mountain.

technology: A method that uses science to solve problems and the tools used to solve those problems.

tourism: The business of drawing in tourists, or people traveling to visit another place.

INDEX

WEBSITES

Due to the changing nature of Internet links, PowerKids Press has developed an online list of websites related to the subject of this book. This site is updated regularly. Please use this link to access the list: www.powerkidslinks.com/EHTR/atolls